DOVER GAME AND PUZZLE ACTIVITY BOOKS

Riddles, Riddles, Riddles

DARWIN A. HINDMAN

Illustrations by Larry Daste

DOVER PUBLICATIONS, INC.
Mineola, New York

Bibliographical Note

This Dover edition, first published in 1997, is a new selection of riddles from *1800 Riddles, Enigmas and Conundrums*, published by Dover Publications, Inc., New York, in 1963. Illustrations by Larry Daste have been added to this edition.

Library of Congress Cataloging-in-Publication Data

Hindman, Darwin Alexander.
   [1800 riddles, enigmas, and conundrums]
   Riddles, riddles, riddles / Darwin A. Hindman ; illustrated by Larry Daste.
     p.   cm.
   Originally published: 1800 riddles, enigmas, and conundrums. New York ; Dover Publications, 1963.
   ISBN-13: 978-0-486-29654-8 (pbk.)
   ISBN-10: 0-486-29654-7 (pbk.)
   1. Riddles. I. Title.
PN6371.H53   1997
818'.02—dc21   96-54023
                                      CIP

Manufactured in the United States by RR Donnelley
29654712   2015
www.doverpublications.com

Contents

The Animal Kingdom

Why would a compliment from a chicken be an insult?
ANS: Because it would be fowl language.

What does a hen do when she stands on one foot?
ANS: Lifts up the other.

Why are a rooster's feathers always smooth?
ANS: Because he carries a fine comb.

What did the little chick say when it found an orange in its nest?
ANS: "Oh, look at the orange Mama laid."

Why is a turkey like a ghost?
ANS: Because he's always a-gobblin'.

What does every duckling become when it first takes to water?
ANS: It becomes wet.

What geometrical figure represents a lost parrot?
ANS: Polygon.

Why is the flight of an eagle a most unpleasant sight?
ANS: Because it's an 'igh soar.

Why must birds in a nest always agree?
ANS: To keep from falling out.

Why do birds clean out a fruit tree so quickly?
ANS: *Because they take away a peck at a time.*

Why are birds melancholy in the morning?
ANS: *Because their little bills are all over dew.*

If you saw a bird sitting on a twig, how could you get the twig without disturbing the bird?
ANS: *Wait until the bird flew away.*

What bird can lift the heaviest weight?
ANS: *The crane.*

How do we know that one bird is insane?
ANS: *Because he's always a raven.*

Why is a dog's tail like the heart of a tree?
ANS: *Because it is farthest from the bark.*

Why is a dog biting his own tail a good manager?
ANS: *Because he makes both ends meet.*

When is a dog's tail not a dog's tail?
ANS: *When it's a-waggin'.*

If a dog should lose his tail, where would he go to get another?
ANS: *To Sears and Roebuck, where everything is retailed.*

Why is a lame dog like a boy adding six and seven?
ANS: *Because he puts down three and carries one.*

When is a yellow dog most likely to enter a house?
ANS: *When the door is open.*

Why is a dog dressed warmer in summer than in winter?
ANS: *Because in winter he wears a fur coat, while in summer he wears a coat, and pants.*

What animal is more wonderful than a counting dog?
ANS: *A spelling bee.*

Why is a cat like a transcontinental highway?
ANS: *Because it's fur from one end to the other.*

Why does a cat sleep more comfortably in summer than in winter?
ANS: Because summer brings the cat-er-pillar.

What do people in Tennessee call little gray cats?
ANS: Kittens.

Prove that a cat has three tails.
ANS: No cat has two tails. One cat has one more tail than no cat. Therefore one cat has three tails.

What is the principal part of a horse?
ANS: The mane part.

Why is a colt like an egg?
ANS: Because it can't be used until it is broken.

Why should one never gossip in a stable?
ANS: Because all horses carry tails.

How is it that a horse has six legs?
ANS: He has forelegs in front and two legs behind.

> Thirty-two white horses on a red hill;
> Now they stamp, now they champ,
> Now they stand still.

ANS: The teeth.

How could a horse be like a bird?
ANS: Didn't you ever see a horse-fly?

Why do goldfish always seem so well traveled?
ANS: Because they all have been around the globe.

What is the best way to keep fish from smelling?
ANS: Cut off their noses.

Why should fish be well educated?
ANS: Because they are commonly found in schools.

Why should a fisherman always be wealthy?
ANS: Because all his profit is net profit.

When is a wall like a fish?
ANS: When it is scaled.

Why did the lobster blush?
ANS: *Because he saw the salad dressing.*

What is worse than finding a worm in an apple?
ANS: *Finding half a worm.*

What are the largest ants?
ANS: *Giants.*

When did the fly fly?
ANS: *When the spider spied her.*

Why is it that mosquitoes cannot annoy a man while he is asleep?
ANS: *Because they wake him up first, and then annoy him.*

How do we know that mosquitoes are happy?
ANS: *They always sing at their work.*

How do mosquitoes show that they are religious?
ANS: *First they sing over you, and then they prey upon you.*

Can you tell me how long cows should be milked?
ANS: *In the same way as short ones.*

When is a cow not a cow?
ANS: *When she is turned into a pasture.*

Which has more legs, a cow or no cow?
ANS: *No cow; a cow has four legs, but no cow has eight legs.*

Why does a baby pig eat so much?
ANS: *To make a hog of himself.*

Why is a pig in the house like a house afire?
ANS: *Because the sooner it is put out the better.*

What makes more noise than a pig caught in a fence?
ANS: *Two pigs caught in a fence.*

Why is a pig the most remarkable animal in the farmyard?
ANS: *Because he is first killed and then cured.*

Why do white sheep eat so much more than black ones?
ANS: *Because there are so many more of them.*

Why does a cow go over a hill?
ANS: *Because she can't go under it.*

How does a camel appear stubborn?
ANS: *He always has his back up.*

Would you rather an elephant attacked you or a gorilla?
ANS: *I'd rather he attacked the gorilla.*

Why has the giraffe such a long neck?
ANS: *Because his head is so far from his body.*

What is worse than a giraffe with a sore throat?
ANS: *A centipede with sore feet.*

What do hippopotamuses have that no other animals have?
ANS: *Baby hippopotamuses.*

When is a man like a snake?
ANS: *When he is rattled.*

What makes a squirrel run up a tree?
ANS: *Aw, nuts!*

Why should a turtle be pitied?
ANS: *Because his is a hard case.*

A frog, a duck, and a skunk all went to town to see the circus. Did they all get in or not?
ANS: *No. The frog got in because he had a green back, and the duck got in because he had a bill, but the skunk did not get in because all he had was a scent, and it was a bad one.*

What animal doesn't play fair?
ANS: *Cheetah.*

What animal never grows old?
ANS: *Gnu.*

What animal do you think of when you hear a fish story?
ANS: *Lion.*

What animal would you like to be on a cold day?
ANS: *A little otter.*

If a well-known animal you behead,
A larger one you will have instead.
ANS: Fox—ox.

What animal drops from the clouds?
ANS: The rain, dear.

Old Testament Teasers

Who was the most popular actor in the Bible?
ANS: Samson; he brought down the house.

Who was the most successful physician in the Bible?
ANS: Job; he had the most patience.

Who was the fastest runner in the Bible?
ANS: Adam; he was first in the human race.

Who was the straightest man in the Bible?
ANS: Joseph; Pharaoh made a ruler of him.

Who was the strongest man in the Bible?
ANS: Jonah; the whale couldn't keep him down.

Who was the first great financier in the Bible?
ANS: Noah; he floated his stock while the whole world was in liquidation.

What three noblemen are mentioned in the Bible?
ANS: Barren fig tree, Lord how long, and Count thy blessings.

At what time of day was Adam born?
ANS: A little before Eve.

Why had Eve no fear of the measles?
ANS: Because she'd Adam.

What did Adam first plant in the Garden of Eden?
ANS: His foot.

Why did Adam bite the apple that Eve gave to him?
ANS: Because he had no knife.

What did Adam and Eve do when they were expelled from the Garden of Eden?
ANS: They raised Cain.

How many apples were eaten in the Garden of Eden?
ANS: Eleven: Eve ate, and Adam too, and the Devil won.

How do we know that Cain was an enemy of President Lincoln?
ANS: Because he hated Abe-L.

How long did Cain hate his brother?
ANS: As long as he was Abel.

How were Adam and Eve prevented from gambling?
ANS: Their paradise (pair o' dice) was taken away from them.

Where was Noah when the lights went out?
ANS: In d' ark.

In what order did Noah come from the ark?
ANS: He came forth.

Why could nobody play cards on the ark?
ANS: Because Noah sat on the deck.

Why did not the worms, like other creatures, go into the ark in pairs?
ANS: Because they went in apples.

Where did Noah strike the first nail in the ark?
ANS: On the head.

Anatomy of a Riddle

Why can two slender persons not become great friends?
ANS: Because they must always be slight acquaintances.

What is the best way to get fat?
ANS: Go to the butcher shop.

When is a doctor most annoyed?
ANS: When he is out of patients.

What kind of doctor would a duck become?
ANS: A quack doctor.

Why should a doctor be less likely than other people to be upset on the ocean?
ANS: Because he is accustomed to see sickness.

Why is a doctor the meanest man on earth?
ANS: Because he treats you and then makes you pay for it.

How do we know that a dentist is unhappy at his work?
ANS: Because he always looks down in the mouth.

Why is a dead doctor like a dead duck?
ANS: Because he has done quacking.

Why wouldn't Mother let the doctor operate on Father?
ANS: Because she didn't want anybody else to open her male.

What is the best thing to take when you are run down?
ANS: *The number of the car that hit you.*

Why did the moron always tiptoe past the medicine cabinet?
ANS: *He didn't want to awaken the sleeping pills.*

Why does your sense of touch suffer when you are ill?
ANS: *Because you don't feel well.*

Why would a sixth sense be a handicap?
ANS: *Because it would be a new sense.*

Why is a nail in an oak log like a sick person?
ANS: *Because it's in firm.*

A knight in shining armor had a pain. Tell me in one sentence when it was and where it was.
ANS: *It was in the middle of the night (knight).*

Why is a bad cold a great humiliation?
ANS: *Because it brings the proudest man to his sneeze.*

Why does a bald-headed man have no use for keys?
ANS: *Because he has lost his locks.*

Why do women not become bald as soon as men?
ANS: *Because they wear their hair longer.*

Why do women put their hair in rollers?
ANS: *To wake curly in the morning.*

Why isn't your nose twelve inches long?
ANS: *Because if it were it would be a foot.*

What is the cheapest feature of the face?
ANS: *Nostrils; they are two for a scent.*

Why is the nose in the middle of the face?
ANS: *Because it is the scenter.*

Why can you not remember the last tooth that you had pulled?
ANS: *Because it went right out of your head.*

Why can a blind man see his father?
ANS: *Because his father is always a parent.*

What should you always do with your eyes?
ANS: Dot them.

What has five eyes, but cannot see?
ANS: The Mississippi River.

What is it that by losing an eye has nothing left but a nose?
ANS: The word NOISE.

Why are Panama hats like deaf people?
ANS: Because you can't make them here.

When do elephants have eight feet?
ANS: When there are two of them.

What has four legs and a back, but no body?
ANS: A chair.

What has a hundred legs but cannot walk?
ANS: Fifty pairs of pants.

What has four legs and flies?
ANS: A dead horse.

What else has four legs and flies?
ANS: Two pairs of pants.

What has eighteen legs and catches flies?
ANS: A baseball team.

What has four legs and flies in the air?
ANS: Two birds.

What has a foot on each end and one in the middle?
ANS: A yardstick.

What did the big toe say to the little toe?
ANS: "There's a heel following us."

Why did the moron cut his fingers off?
ANS: Because he wanted to write shorthand.

What do you call a man who doesn't have all his fingers on one hand?
ANS: Perfectly normal, for his fingers are properly divided between his two hands.

Fads and Fashions

One morning a boy couldn't find his trousers; what did he do?
ANS: He raced around the room until he was breathing in short pants.

Why did George Washington wear red-white-and-blue suspenders?
ANS: To hold his pants up.

What does the evening wear?
ANS: The close of day.

Why does a coat get larger when it is taken out of a suitcase?
ANS: Because when you take it out you find it in creases.

What is always at the head of fashion, yet always out of date?
ANS: The letter F.

What member of Congress wears the largest hat?
ANS: The one with the largest head.

What makes a pair of shoes?
ANS: Two shoes.

Which one of our Presidents wore the largest shoes?
ANS: The one with the biggest feet.

When a shoemaker makes a shoe, what is the first thing that he uses?
ANS: *The last.*

When is a pair of shoes like a dying man?
ANS: *When the sole is departing from the body.*

What is the latest thing in dresses?
ANS: *A nightdress.*

What kind of dress lasts longest?
ANS: *A housedress, for it is never worn out.*

What kind of umbrella does the President's wife carry on a rainy day?
ANS: *A wet one.*

Three large women went walking under one umbrella, but none of them got wet. Why?
ANS: *It wasn't raining.*

What is the biggest jewel in the world?
ANS: *A baseball diamond.*

Why is a cannon like a vanity case?
ANS: *Because it is useless without powder.*

What is appropriate material for a bald man to wear?
ANS: *Mo'-hair.*

What is appropriate material for a banker to wear?
ANS: *Checks, or cashmere.*

What is appropriate material for a dairyman to wear?
ANS: *Cheesecloth.*

What is appropriate material for a fat man to wear?
ANS: *Broadcloth.*

What is appropriate material for a filling-station operator to wear?
ANS: *Oilcloth.*

What is appropriate material for a musician to wear?
ANS: *Organdy.*

From Soup to Nuts

What would happen to a man if he swallowed his teaspoon?
ANS: He wouldn't be able to stir.

Why should a greedy man wear a plaid vest?
ANS: To keep a check on his stomach.

Is it safe to write a letter on an empty stomach?
ANS: It is safe enough, but it is better to write the letter on paper.

Why did the moron eat dynamite?
ANS: He wanted his hair to grow out in bangs.

In what country were the first doughnuts fried?
ANS: In Greece.

What made the tart tart?
ANS: She didn't want the baker to bake her.

Why is a loaf of bread four weeks old like a mouse running into a hole?
ANS: Because you can see it's stale.

Why did the moron go into the street with his bread and butter?
ANS: He was looking for the traffic jam.

Why did the jelly roll?
ANS: *It saw the apple turnover.*

Why is a promise like an egg?
ANS: *Because it is so easily broken.*

If cheese comes after dinner, what comes after cheese?
ANS: *A mouse.*

Why did the little moron take sugar and cream with him to the movie?
ANS: *He heard there was going to be a serial.*

What kind of jam cannot be eaten?
ANS: *A traffic jam.*

What did the candy bar say to the lollipop?
ANS: *"Hello, sucker."*

What did the mayonnaise say to the refrigerator?
ANS: *"Please close the door; I'm dressing."*

When does a cook not prepare a square meal?
ANS: *When she wants it to go round.*

Why is a baker like a beggar?
ANS: *Because he kneads bread.*

Why are fishermen and shepherds not to be trusted?
ANS: *Because they live by hook and by crook.*

If a waiter were carrying a turkey on a platter and let it fall, what three great national calamities would occur?
ANS: *The downfall of turkey, the breaking up of china, and the overthrow of grease.*

What beverage is appropriate for a cowboy?
ANS: *Brandy.*

What beverage is appropriate for a golfer?
ANS: *Tea.*

What beverage is appropriate for a prize fighter?
ANS: Punch.

What beverage is appropriate for a sailor?
ANS: Port.

With which hand should you stir your cocoa?
ANS: With either, but it is better to stir it with a spoon.

Why should a poor man drink coffee?
ANS: Because he has no proper-ty.

What beverage represents what the patient has and what the doctor gets?
ANS: Cof-fee.

What beverage represents the beginning of time?
ANS: Tea. (T).

Why is fresh milk like something that never happened?
ANS: Because it hasn't a curd.

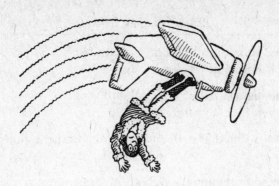

The Sky's the Limit

What part of London is in France?
ANS: The letter N.

Why should we not believe one word that comes from Holland?
ANS: Because Holland is such a low-lying country.

Why doesn't Sweden export cattle?
ANS: Because she wants to keep her Stockholm.

Why is the map of Europe like a frying pan?
ANS: Because it has Greece on the bottom.

If a thin man were to dress himself in the clothes of a tall, fat man, what two cities of France would he resemble?
ANS: Toulon and Toulouse.

Why should you not swim in the river at Paris?
ANS: Because if you did you would be in Seine.

What is the happiest state in the union?
ANS: Merry land.

If Miss Issippi should lend Miss Ouri her New Jersey, what would Dela-ware?
ANS: I don't know, but Alaska.

How do sailors identify Long Island?
ANS: By the sound.

What would you do if you found Chicago, Ill.?
ANS: *Call a Baltimore M-d.*

What is the highest public building in Boston?
ANS: *The public library has the most stories.*

Which state is round at both ends and high in the middle?
ANS: *O-hi-o.*

What is found in the middle of both America and Australia?
ANS: *The letter R.*

If a man is born in Turkey, grows up in Italy, comes to America, and dies in Chicago, what is he?
ANS: *Dead.*

Is there much difference between the North Pole and the South Pole?
ANS: *Yes, all the difference in the world.*

What country makes you shiver?
ANS: *Chile.*

With the name of a country, tell what the mother asked her crying child.
ANS: *Are you Hungary?*

What did the child reply?
ANS: *Yes, Siam.*

What did the mother say next?
ANS: *Come along, then, I'll Fiji.*

What did she give him to eat?
ANS: *A slice of Turkey.*

Why did the child start crying again?
ANS: *He wanted Samoa.*

What did the mother say that time?
ANS: *Stop those Wales.*

What river is ever without a beginning and ending?
ANS: *Severn; S-ever-N.*

What holds the moon up?
ANS: *The moon-beams.*

Why can the world never come to an end?
ANS: *Because it is round.*

If I were in the sun and U (you) were out of the sun, what would the sun become?
ANS: *Sin.*

When will water stop running downhill?
ANS: *When it reaches the bottom.*

When does water resemble a gymnast?
ANS: *When it makes a spring.*

Which moves faster, heat or cold?
ANS: *Heat, for you can catch cold.*

When is the weather worst for rats and mice?
ANS: *When it rains cats and dogs.*

What always happens at the end of a dry spell?
ANS: *It rains.*

What is worse than raining cats and dogs?
ANS: *Hailing taxicabs.*

Why is a heavy snowfall easily understood?
ANS: *Because one can see the drift.*

Of Princes, Politicians
and Pilferers

Why are the Middle Ages called the Dark Ages?
ANS: Because there were so many knights then.

Captain Cook made three voyages around the world and was killed on one of these voyages. On which one?
ANS: The last one.

Why would you prefer the death of Joan of Arc to that of Mary, Queen of Scots?
ANS: Because a hot steak is preferable to a cold chop.

Why was a medieval tournament like sleep?
ANS: Because it was a knightly occupation.

What did Paul Revere say when he finished his famous ride?
ANS: "Whoa."

Where are kings usually crowned?
ANS: On the head.

Why is it wise for a king to have several court jesters?
ANS: Because in that way he always keeps his wits about him.

Why is the Prince of Wales like a cloudy day?
ANS: Because he is likely to reign.

Why is a man who gets knocked down at an election like the world that we inhabit?
ANS: Because he is flattened at the polls.

Why can't a deaf man be legally convicted?
ANS: Because it is unlawful to condemn a man without a hearing.

Why is a professional thief comfortable?
ANS: Because he takes things easy.

What is the least dangerous kind of robbery?
ANS: Safe robbery.

Why is a thief like a tired man?
ANS: Because he needs arresting.

Why can a thief be said to be broadminded?
ANS: Because he is open to conviction.

Why is a thief called a jailbird?
ANS: Because he has been a-robbin'.

Why is a man in jail like a boat full of water?
ANS: Because he requires bailing out.

Backyard, Churchyard, Schoolyard

What is all over the house?
ANS: The roof.

What runs all around the yard without moving?
ANS: The fence.

What did the chimney and the door do when the house caught on fire?
ANS: The chimney flue and the door bolted.

What did one wall say to the other wall?
ANS: "I'll meet you at the corner."

What did the rug say to the floor?
ANS: "Hands up; I've got you covered."

What relation is a door-mat to a door-step?
ANS: A step-fa'ther.

When is a door not a door?
ANS: When it's ajar.

When should a window pane blush?
ANS: When it sees the weather-strip.

What will go up the chimney down and down the chimney down, but will not go up the chimney up nor down the chimney up?
ANS: An umbrella.

Why must chimney sweeping be a very agreeable business?
ANS: Because it soots everyone who tries it.

When does a chair dislike you?
ANS: When it can't bear you.

When is a chair like a woman's dress?
ANS: When it is sat-in.

Why did the moron sleep on the chandelier?
ANS: Because he was a light sleeper.

Why is a mirror like a resolution?
ANS: Because it is so easily broken.

How many sides has a pitcher?
ANS: Two; outside and inside.

Which burns longer, a wax candle or a tallow candle?
ANS: Neither; they both burn shorter.

What happens to a lighted match when you drop it into a river?
ANS: It goes out.

Why is an empty matchbox superior to all other boxes?
ANS: Because it is matchless.

Why are many sermons like asparagus?
ANS: Because it is the ends of them that people enjoy most.

Why are church bells the most obedient of inanimate objects?
ANS: Because they make a noise whenever they are tolled.

If the Devil were to lose his tail, where should he go to get another?
ANS: To a liquor store, where bad spirits are retailed.

What's in the church, but not the steeple?
The parson has it, but not the people.
ANS: The letter R.

What changes the lower regions into the flower regions?
ANS: The letter F.

On the desk of a certain country schoolteacher is a bell which she uses for signaling class periods. You've been told the teacher's name. What is it?
ANS: Isabel.

Readin' and Writin' in Riddle

Why are people who write books so funny looking?
ANS: Because their tales come right out of their heads.

Why are the pages of a book like the days of man?
ANS: Because they are numbered.

When is an apple like a book?
ANS: When it is red.

What is the difference between a book and a bore?
ANS: You can shut up a book.

Why should "Watermelon" be a good name for a newspaper?
ANS: Because its insides would be sure to be red.

Why does Santa Claus always go down the chimney?
ANS: Because it soots him.

How did Little Bo-peep lose her sheep?
ANS: She had a crook with her.

Do you say, "Nine and five *are* thirteen" or "Nine and five *is* thirteen"?
ANS: Neither, for nine and five are fourteen.

In what sort of syllables ought a parrot to speak?
ANS: In polly-syllables.

How would you punctuate this sentence: "I saw a five-dollar bill on the street"?
ANS: I would make a dash after it.

Why is whispering prohibited in company?
ANS: Because it is not aloud.

What can you break with a whisper more easily than with a hammer?
ANS: A secret.

Ask a question that must be answered "Yes."
ANS: "What does Y-E-S spell?"

Ask a question that cannot be answered "Yes."
ANS: "Are you asleep?"

How can a man tell the naked truth?
ANS: By giving the bare facts.

Why is a lie like a wig?
ANS: Because it is a false-hood.

Love and Marriage

Who are the largest two ladies in the United States?
ANS: Miss Ouri and Mrs. Sippi.

How would you measure a lover's sincerity?
ANS: By his sighs.

Why should one never kiss in a vegetable garden?
ANS: Because the potatoes have eyes, the corn has ears, and the beanstalk.

Why is a bride always unlucky on her wedding day?
ANS: Because she does not marry the best man.

If two San Francisco telegraph operators were married, what would they become?
ANS: A Western Union.

> Pray tell me, ladies, if you can,
> Who is that highly favored man,
> Who though he has married many a wife,
> May still be single all his life?

ANS: A clergyman.

Why is a kiss over the telephone like a straw hat?
ANS: Because it's not felt.

What is the best name for the wife of an astronomer?
ANS: Stella.

What is the best name for the wife of a dancing master?
ANS: Grace.

What is the best name for the wife of a doctor?
ANS: Patience.

What is the best name for the wife of a gambler?
ANS: Betty.

What is the best name for the wife of a jeweler?
ANS: Ruby.

What is the best name for the wife of a lawyer?
ANS: Sue.

What is the best name for the wife of a marksman?
ANS: Amy.

Why does a wife hug her husband?
ANS: Because she wants to get around him.

Why is a room packed with married people like an empty room?
ANS: Because there is not a single person in it.

Why does a spinster wear cotton gloves?
ANS: Because she hasn't any kids.

Why is a single person like borrowed money?
ANS: Because he is alone.

"That's Entertainment!"

Why are pianos so noble?
ANS: Because they are upright, grand, and square.

A man was locked in a room which had nothing in it except a piano.
How did he get out?
ANS: He played the piano until he found the right key.

How do we know that phonographs have been to jail?
ANS: They all have records.

What is the best musical motto?
ANS: B-sharp and B-natural, but never B-flat.

What musical key cannot vote?
ANS: A-minor.

Why are sidewalks in winter like music?
ANS: Because if you don't C-sharp, you will B-flat.

What pets make the loudest music?
ANS: Trum-pets.

What does an artist best like to draw?
ANS: His salary.

Why is a bad picture like weak tea?
ANS: Because it is not well drawn.

Why are photographers the most uncivil of people?
ANS: *Because when we make application for a copy of our portrait, they always reply with a negative.*

Why is a theater such a sad place?
ANS: *Because all the seats are in tiers.*

What is the coldest place in a theater?
ANS: *Z-row.*

Why is it hard to get a baseball game started in the afternoon?
ANS: *Because the bats like to sleep in the daytime.*

Why is a baseball game like a cake?
ANS: *Because its success depends on the batter.*

Why is a baseball game like yesterday?
ANS: *Because it is a pastime.*

How can a baseball game end in a score of four to two without a man reaching first base?
ANS: *The players are all women.*

Why did Babe Ruth and Lou Gehrig make so much money?
ANS: *Because a good batter makes good dough.*

Why is tennis such a noisy game?
ANS: *Because every player raises a racket.*

What animal do you look like when you go in swimming?
ANS: *A little bare.*

What did the big firecracker say to the little firecracker?
ANS: *"My pop's bigger than your pop."*

Why is dancing like new milk?
ANS: *Because it strengthens the calves.*

Why are playing cards like wolves?
ANS: *Because they come in packs.*

Why is a group of convicts like a deck of cards?
ANS: *Because there is a knave in every suit.*

Why is a joke less durable than a church bell?
ANS: Because after it has been told a few times it is worn out.

Why is a poor joke like a broken pencil?
ANS: Because it has no point.

Why is a joke like a coconut?
ANS: Because it's no good until it is cracked.

Why is it best to tell a story with a hammer?
ANS: To make it more striking.

Why do people laugh up their sleeves?
ANS: Because that is where their funnybones are.

I know something that will tickle you. What?
ANS: A feather.

Why is a crossword puzzle like a quarrel?
ANS: Because one word leads to another.

Did you ever hear the story of the red-hot poker?
ANS: You couldn't grasp it.

Did you ever hear the story about the two holes in the ground?
ANS: Well, well.

Did you ever hear the story of the new roof?
ANS: It's over your head.

Did you ever hear the story of the dirty window?
ANS: You couldn't see through it.

Funny Money

Which is more valuable, a paper dollar or a silver dollar?
ANS: The paper dollar, because when you put it into your pocket you double it, and when you take it out you find it in creases.

Which is better, an old five-dollar bill or a new one?
ANS: Any five-dollar bill is better than a one-dollar bill.

Why is a penny like a rooster on a fence?
ANS: Because its head is on one side and its tail on the other.

A nickel and a dime were crossing a bridge and the nickel fell off. Why didn't the dime fall too?
ANS: Because it had more cents than the nickel.

Why is an empty purse always the same?
ANS: Because there is never any change in it.

What coin doubles in value when half is deducted?
ANS: A half dollar.

What is the difference between a new five-cent piece and an old-fashioned quarter?
ANS: Twenty cents.

What is the debtor's favorite tree?
ANS: The will-owe.

What is the surest way to double your dollar?
ANS: Fold it.

Why should you ride a mule if you want to get rich?
ANS: Because you are no sooner on than you are better off.

Why do bankers always hear the latest financial news?
ANS: Because they have cash-iers.

What kind of face does an auctioneer like best?
ANS: One that is for bidding.

Why was the moron able to buy ice at half price?
ANS: Because it was melted.

If a ton of coal costs $6.50, what will a cord of firewood come to?
ANS: Ashes.

If you can buy eight eggs for twenty-six cents, how many can you buy for a cent and a quarter?
ANS: Eight.

If butter is fifty cents a pound in Chicago, what are windowpanes in Detroit?
ANS: Glass.

What do you call a man who is always wiring for money?
ANS: An electrician.

The Garden Variety

What did the big rose say to the little rose?
ANS: "Hiya, Bud."

When the poet asked the woodman to "spare that tree," why did he expect his request to be granted?
ANS: Because he knew the woodman was a good feller.

What ailment is the oak tree most subject to?
ANS: A corn.

What tree bears the most toothsome fruit?
ANS: Dentistry.

If you should plant a puppy, what kind of tree would come up?
ANS: A dogwood.

How can you make fifteen bushels of corn from one bushel of corn?
ANS: Pop it.

If a farmer can raise fifty bushels of corn in dry weather, what can he raise in wet weather?
ANS: An umbrella.

How far can you go into the woods?
ANS: As far as the middle; after that you will be going out.

How did the garden laugh at the gardener?
ANS: *It said, "Hoe, hoe."*

Why is it more dangerous to go to the woods in the spring than at any other time?
ANS: *Because in the spring the grass has blades, the flowers have pistils, the leaves shoot, the cowslips about, and the bulrush is out.*

If Bob had a whole apple and Tom had only a bite, what should Tom do?
ANS: *Scratch it.*

What is the reddest side of an apple?
ANS: *The outside.*

How can you divide nineteen apples absolutely equally among seven small boys?
ANS: *Make them into applesauce, and measure it out very carefully.*

When are two apples alike?
ANS: *When they are pared.*

When an apple wanted to fight a banana, why did the banana run away?
ANS: *Because it was yellow.*

What did the mother strawberry say to the baby strawberry?
ANS: *"Junior, don't get into a jam."*

What is the largest vegetable?
ANS: *A policeman's beat.*

What vegetable needs a plumber?
ANS: *Leek.*

Why is an onion like a ringing bell?
ANS: *Because peel follows peel.*

How many peas in a pint?
ANS: *One P.*

"Timing Is Everything"

What part of a clock has been used before?
ANS: Second hand.

How long will an eight-day clock run without winding?
ANS: It won't run at all without winding.

Why does a clock never strike thirteen?
ANS: It hasn't the face to do so.

If a man should smash a clock, would he be accused of killing time?
ANS: Not if the clock struck first.

Why should a clock never be placed at the head of the stairs?
ANS: Because it might run down and strike one.

When is a very angry man like a clock showing fifty-nine minutes past twelve?
ANS: When he is just about to strike one.

Why did the moron throw his clock out the window?
ANS: He liked to see time fly.

Why should you always carry a watch when crossing a desert?
ANS: Because it has a spring in it.

When is it difficult to get one's watch out of one's pocket?
ANS: *When it's ticking there.*

What time is it when the clock strikes thirteen?
ANS: *Time to have the clock repaired.*

If a man should give one son fifteen cents and another ten cents, what time would it be?
ANS: *A quarter to two.*

What time is it when you see a monkey scratching with his left hand?
ANS: *Five after one.*

What time is it when a pie is equally divided among four hungry boys?
ANS: *A quarter to one.*

If the postmaster went to the circus and a lion ate him, what time would it be?
ANS: *Ate P.M. (eight P.M.).*

At what time by the clock is a pun most effective?
ANS: *When it strikes one.*

What is a good way to kill time in the winter?
ANS: *Sleigh it.*

Why is it that there is not a moment that we can call our own?
ANS: *Because the minutes are not hours.*

What is the best way to make the hours go fast?
ANS: *Use the spur of the moment.*

What animal keeps the best time?
ANS: *A watchdog.*

Which is the strongest day of the week?
ANS: *Sunday, because all the rest are week-days.*

Where does Friday come before Thursday?
ANS: *In the dictionary.*

What is the best day for making pancakes?
ANS: Fri-day.

When day breaks, what becomes of the pieces?
ANS: They go into morning.

Why is there no such thing as a whole day?
ANS: Because every day begins by breaking.

What day of the year is a command to go forward?
ANS: March fourth.

Why should soldiers be especially tired on the first of April?
ANS: Because they have just finished a March of thirty-one days.

How many weeks belong to the year?
ANS: Forty-six; the other six are only Lent.

In what month do people talk the least?
ANS: In the shortest month, February.

On the Tracks, On the Sea, On the Road

Why does a freight car need no locomotive?
ANS: Because the freight makes the cargo.

Why should one never complain about the price of a railroad ticket?
ANS: Because it is a fare thing.

Why is a railroad exceedingly patriotic?
ANS: Because it is bound to the country with the strongest ties.

What ship has two mates but no captain?
ANS: Courtship.

What ship is always managed by more than one person?
ANS: Partnership.

When does a boat show affection?
ANS: When it hugs the shore.

What comes with an auto, is of no use to an auto, and yet the auto cannot run without it?
ANS: Noise.

What is the hardest thing about learning to ride a bicycle?
ANS: The pavement.

Why do taxi drivers prefer tall women passengers to short ones?
ANS: Because the higher the fare, the better they like it.

Why are coachmen like clouds?
ANS: *Because they hold the reins.*

What do you always notice running along the streets in a town?
ANS: *The curb.*

What makes a road broad?
ANS: *The letter B.*

Why can we send no more dispatches to Washington?
ANS: *Because he is dead.*

If a telephone and a piece of paper should run a race, which would win?
ANS: *The telephone, because the paper would always remain stationery.*

Why is a news broadcaster like an Irish vegetable?
ANS: *Because he is a commentator.*

What did one little ink drop ask another little ink drop?
ANS: *Are all your relatives in the pen too?*

"The World's a Stage"

Why is a newborn babe like a little dog's tail?
ANS: *Because it was never seen before.*

Have you ever heard of a baby raised on elephant's milk?
ANS: *Yes, a baby elephant.*

Who is bigger, Mrs. Bigger or her baby?
ANS: *The baby is a little Bigger.*

Why is a dirty child like flannel?
ANS: *Because it shrinks from washing.*

Whom do children dislike the most?
ANS: *The women who bore them.*

Why is a barefooted boy like an Eskimo?
ANS: *Because he wears no shoes.*

Who earns his living without doing a day's work?
ANS: *A night watchman.*

What man's business is best when things are dullest?
ANS: *A knife sharpener.*

Why may carpenters reasonably believe there is no such thing as stone?
ANS: *Because they never saw it.*

41

When are electricians most successful?
ANS: When they make good connections.

How could a good fireman lose his job?
ANS: He might go to blazes too fast.

Why is a real-estate man not a man of words?
ANS: Because he's a man of deeds.

What kind of servants are best for hotels?
ANS: The inn-experienced.

Why are soldiers in the U.S. Army not going to have bayonets any longer?
ANS: Because they are long enough.

When is a soldier not a whole soldier?
ANS: When he is in quarters.

Why must a dishonest man stay indoors?
ANS: So no one will ever find him out.

When is it a good thing to lose your temper?
ANS: When it is a bad one.

Three copycats were sitting on a cliff and one jumped off. How many were left?
ANS: None, because they were all copycats.

If you woke up in the night feeling sad, what would you do?
ANS: Look on the bed for a comforter.

What is the best way to keep loafers from standing on street corners?
ANS: Give them chairs and let them sit down.

When does a timid girl turn to stone?
ANS: When she becomes a little bolder.

Why should you always remain calm when you encounter cannibals?
ANS: It is better not to get into a stew.

Where can you always find sympathy?
ANS: In the dictionary.

Where does charity begin?
ANS: *At C (sea).*

If a girl falls into a well, why can her brother not help her out?
ANS: *Because he cannot be a brother and assist her too.*

Why did the moron lock his father in the refrigerator?
ANS: *Because he likes cold pop.*

Two Indians are standing on a hill, and one is the father of the other's son. What relation are the two Indians to each other?
ANS: *Husband and wife.*

What is everyone in the world doing at the same time?
ANS: *Growing older.*

When is it easiest to see through a man?
ANS: *When he has a pain in his stomach.*

What is the best way to turn people's heads?
ANS: *Go to church late.*

What kind of paper tells you who you are?
ANS: *Tissue.*

How can you get into a locked cemetery at night?
ANS: *Use a skeleton key.*

What did the moron do when he thought he was dying?
ANS: *He moved to the living room.*

Paradoxes A-Plenty

What is big enough to hold a pig and small enough to hold in your hand?
ANS: *A pen.*

What is it from which you may take away the whole and still have some left, or take away some and have the whole left?
ANS: *The word WHOLESOME.*

What goes farther the slower it goes?
ANS: *Money.*

What goes from New York to Albany without moving?
ANS: *The highway.*

What is always coming but never arrives?
ANS: *Tomorrow.*

What always remains down even when it flies up in the air?
ANS: *A feather.*

What is it that you cannot hold ten minutes, even though it is lighter than a feather?
ANS: *Your breath.*

What is it that no one wishes to have, yet no one wishes to lose?
ANS: *A bald head.*

What is it that everyone requires, that everyone gives, that everyone asks, and that very few take?
ANS: *Advice.*

What is it that was given to you, belongs to you exclusively, and yet is used more by your friends than by yourself?
ANS: *Your name.*

What is it that someone else has to take before you can get it?
ANS: *Your photograph.*

What is full of holes and yet holds water?
ANS: *A sponge.*

What can be right but never wrong?
ANS: *An angle.*

What is always before you, yet you can never see it?
ANS: *Your future.*

How might you be completely sleepless for seven days and still not lack any rest?
ANS: *By sleeping at night.*

What lives on its own substance and dies when it devours itself?
ANS: *A candle.*

As long as I eat, I live; but when I drink, I die.
ANS: *Fire.*

What is it that is put on the table, cut, and passed, but never eaten?
ANS: *A deck of cards.*

What is black and white and red all over?
ANS: *A newspaper.*

What else is black and white and red all over?
ANS: *An embarrassed zebra.*

What gets wetter the more it dries?
ANS: *A towel.*

How can a man fall off a fifty-foot ladder and not be hurt?
ANS: *By falling off the bottom rung.*

What is it that occurs four times in every week, twice in every month, and only once in a year?
ANS: *The letter E.*

When is a man two men?
ANS: *When he is beside himself.*

What is it that you break when you name it?
ANS: *Silence.*

What can be broken without being hit or dropped?
ANS: *A promise.*

What Is It?

What does everyone have that he can always count on?
ANS: His fingers.

What is it that one needs most in the long run?
ANS: His breath.

What do you lose every time you stand up?
ANS: Your lap.

What is hard to beat?
ANS: A drum with a hole in it.

What is true to the last?
ANS: A well-made shoe.

What will stay hot longest in the refrigerator?
ANS: Red pepper.

What always ends everything?
ANS: The letter G.

What is the hardest thing to deal with?
ANS: An old deck of cards.

What is the brightest idea of the day?
ANS: Your eye, dear (idea).

What occurs once in a minute, twice in a moment, and not once in a hundred years?
ANS: *The letter M.*

I am filled every morning and emptied every night, except once a year, when I am filled at night and emptied in the morning. What am I?
ANS: *A stocking.*

What is too much for one, enough for two, but nothing at all for three?
ANS: *A secret.*

What runs around town all day and lies under the bed at night with its tongue hanging out?
ANS: *A shoe.*

If you pull it, it's a cane, but if you push it, it's a tent.
ANS: *An umbrella.*

What should you always keep because nobody else wants it?
ANS: *Your temper.*

Luke had it first, Paul had it last; boys never have it; girls have it but once; Miss Sullivan had it twice in the same place, but when she married Pat Murphy she never had it again.
ANS: *The letter L.*

> The beginning of eternity,
> The end of time and space,
> The beginning of every end,
> The end of every race.

ANS: *The letter E.*

> Little Nancy Etticoat
> Wears a white petticoat
> And a red nose;
> The longer she stands,
> The shorter she grows.

ANS: *A candle.*

What is that walks over the fields all day, and sits in the icebox at night?
ANS: *Milk.*

> Old Mother Twitchett, she had but one eye,
> And a great long tail that she let fly;
> And every time she went through a gap,
> She left a bit of her tail in the trap.

ANS: *A needle and thread.*

What we caught we threw away; what we could not catch, we kept.
ANS: *Fleas. (There is a legend that this riddle was given to the great Homer by a fisherman of Ios, and that Homer's death was a result of his chagrin over being unable to solve it. The story is sometimes attributed to Plutarch, but I have not found it in Plutarch's works.)*

What creature walks in the morning on four feet, at noon upon two, at evening upon three?
ANS: *Man: as a baby on hands and knees, later on his feet, and in the evening of life with a cane. (This is, of course, the famous "Riddle of the Sphinx." The Sphinx [of Thebes] made a practice of proposing this riddle to all who happened to pass, and of killing all who failed to guess it. Nobody guessed the riddle until Oedipus came along. Oedipus guessed the riddle, the Sphinx slew herself, and Oedipus became king of Thebes.)*

Alphabet Soup

What letter is most useful to a deaf woman?
ANS: The letter A, because it makes her hear.

What letter is never found in the alphabet?
ANS: The one you mail.

If all the letters in the alphabet were on a mountaintop, which letter would leave first?
ANS: D would begin the descent.

What letter of the alphabet is necessary to make a shoe?
ANS: The last.

What letter will set one of the heavenly bodies in motion?
ANS: T, because it will make a star start.

What letter travels the greatest distance?
ANS: D, because it goes to the end of the world.

If your mother-in-law were to fall overboard, what letter would suit your wishes?
ANS: Letter B.

What letters are in-visible, but never out of sight?
ANS: I and S.

In the word CLOVES, why are C and S, although separated, closely attached?
ANS: *Because there is LOVE between them.*

Which two letters of the alphabet have nothing between them?
ANS: *N and P; they have O between them.*

How would you express in two letters that you were twice the bulk of your companion?
ANS: *I W.*

What two letters express the most agreeable people in the world?
ANS: *U and I.*

If you asked the alphabet to an afternoon party, which letters could not come until later in the evening?
ANS: *The last six, because they cannot come until after T.*

How can you, with eight letters, tell a girl by the name of Ellen that she is everything that is delightful?
ANS: *U-R-A-B-U-T-L-N.*

When were there only two vowels?
ANS: *In the days of No-A, before U and I were born.*

Why should men avoid the letter A?
ANS: *Because it makes men mean.*

Why is the letter A like noon?
ANS: *Because it's the middle of the day.*

Why is the letter A like honeysuckle?
ANS: *Because it always has a B following it.*

What must I do to the alphabet to remove A from it?
ANS: *B-head it.*

Why are A, E, and U the handsome vowels?
ANS: *Because you can't have beauty without them.*

When did Chicago begin with a C and end with an E?
ANS: *Chicago always began with C and END always began with E.*

When was B the first letter of the alphabet?
ANS: *In the days of No-A.*

Why is the letter B like a hot fire?
ANS: *Because it makes oil boil.*

Why is a teacher of girls like the letter C?
ANS: *She makes lasses into classes.*

Why is the letter C such a frigid letter?
ANS: *Because it's in the middle of ice and it makes old people cold people.*

Why is the letter D like a sailor?
ANS: *Because it follows the C.*

Why did Noah object to the letter D?
ANS: *Because it made the ark dark.*

Why is the letter D like a squalling child?
ANS: *Because it makes Ma mad.*

Why is the letter D like a wedding ring?
ANS: *Because we cannot be wed without it.*

Why is the letter E like death?
ANS: *Because it is the end of life.*

Why is E the most unfortunate letter?
ANS: *Because it is never in cash, always in debt, and never out of danger.*

What ends with E, begins with P, and has a thousand letters?
ANS: *Postoffice.*

Why is the letter F like a fishhook?
ANS: *Because it will make an eel feel.*

Why is the letter G like the sun?
ANS: *Because it is the center of light.*

Why is the letter G like 12 P.M.?
ANS: *Because it is the middle of night.*

Why is a farmer astonished at the letter G?
ANS: Because it converts oats into goats.

Why is the letter N like a pig?
ANS: Because it makes a sty nasty.

Why is the letter O like a neatly kept house?
ANS: Because it is always in order.

Why is a horse like the letter O?
ANS: Because "gee" makes it go.

Why is O the only vowel that is sounded?
ANS: Because all the others are in audible.

Why are the fourteenth and fifteenth letters of the alphabet of more importance than the others?
ANS: Because we cannot get on without them.

Why is the letter R indispensable to friendship?
ANS: Because without it friends would be fiends.

How do we know that S is a scary letter?
ANS: It makes cream scream.

Why is a sewing machine like the letter S?
ANS: Because it makes common needles needless.

Tommy Tucker took two strings and tied two turtles to two tall trees. How many T's in that?
ANS: There are two T's in that.

What starts with T, ends with T, and is full of tea?
ANS: Teapot.

Why is an island like the letter T?
ANS: Because it is in the middle of water.

Why should a boy avoid the letter Y?
ANS: Because it can turn a lad into a lady.

How do you spell blind pig?
ANS: B-L-N-D P-G. You have to spell it that way because a blind pig has no eyes.

England, Ireland, Scotland, Wales,
Monkeys, rats, and wiggle-tails.
Spell that with four letters.
ANS: T-H-A-T.

What word is nearly always pronounced wrong, even by the best scholars?
ANS: The word WRONG.

What word of five letters has six left after you take two away?
ANS: Sixty.

What is the longest word in the English language?
ANS: SMILES, because it has a mile between the first and last letters.

Take two letters from a five-letter word and have one left.
ANS: Stone-one.

What is the longest sentence in the world?
ANS: "Go to prison for life."

Make one word from the letters of NEW DOOR.
ANS: ONE WORD.

Make just one word from these letters: D-E-J-N-O-O-R-S-T-U-W.
ANS: JUST ONE WORD.

Make one word from nine thumps.
ANS: PUNISHMENT.

What is the difference between here and there?
ANS: The letter T.

What odd number when beheaded becomes even?
ANS: Seven (S-even).

When a lady faints, what number will restore her?
ANS: You must bring her 2.

Why is twice ten like twice eleven?
ANS: Because twice ten is twenty, and twice eleven is twenty-two (twenty, too).

How many times may 19 be subtracted from 189?
ANS: *Only one; any subsequent subtraction must be from a smaller number.*

Why should the number 288 never be spoken in refined company?
ANS: *Because it is two gross.*

If two is company and three is a crowd, what are four and five?
ANS: *Nine.*

If I dig a hole two feet square and two feet deep, how much dirt is in the hole?
ANS: *None.*

What's the Difference?

What is the difference between a bare head and a hair bed?
ANS: One flees for shelter, the other is shelter for fleas.

What is the difference between the rear light of an automobile and a book of fiction?
ANS: One is a taillight, the other is a light tale.

What is the difference between a cashier and a schoolmaster?
ANS: One minds the till, the other tills the mind.

What is the difference between a chicken that cannot hold its head up, and seven days?
ANS: The first is a weak one, the other is one week.

What is the difference between a china shop and a furniture store?
ANS: One sells tea sets, the other sells settees.

What is the difference between a crown prince and the water in a fountain?
ANS: One is heir to the throne, the other is thrown to the air.

What is the difference between a dog losing his hair, and a man painting a small building?
ANS: One sheds his coat, the other coats his shed.

What is the difference between an elephant and a flea?
ANS: An elephant can have fleas, but a flea cannot have elephants.

What is the difference between a locomotive engineer and a schoolmaster?
ANS: One minds the train, the other trains the mind.

What is the difference between a farmer and a seamstress?
ANS: One gathers what he sows, the other sews what she gathers.

What is the difference between a good soldier and a fashionable young lady?
ANS: One faces the powder, the other powders the face.

What is the difference between a man struck with amazement, and the tail of a Dalmatian dog?
ANS: One is rooted to the spot, the other is spotted to the root.

What is the difference between a nurse taking a patient's pulse, and a champion runner?
ANS: One records the beats, the other beats the records.

What is the difference between an oak tree and a tight shoe?
ANS: One makes acorns, the other makes corns ache.

What is the difference between an organist and a cold in the head?
ANS: One knows the stops, the other stops the nose.

What is the difference between a person late for a train, and a teacher in a girls' school?
ANS: One misses the train, the other trains the misses.

What is the difference between a pitcher of water, and a man throwing his wife off a bridge?
ANS: One is water in the pitcher, the other is pitch her in the water.

What is the difference between a pugilist and a man with a cold?
ANS: One knows his blows, the other blows his nose.

What is the difference between a professional pianist giving a concert, and a member of his audience?
ANS: One plays for his pay, the other pays for his play.

What is the difference between a pugilist and a lapdog?
ANS: One faces the licks, the other licks the face.

What is the difference between a rejected lover and an accepted one?
ANS: *The former misses the kiss, the latter kisses the miss.*

What is the difference between a chimney sweep and a man in mourning?
ANS: *One is blacked with soot, the other is suited with black.*

What is the difference between a tailor and a groom?
ANS: *One mends a tear, the other tends a mare.*

What is the difference between a winter storm and a child with a cold?
ANS: *In the one it snows, it blows; the other blows its nose.*

What is the difference between a woman and a postage stamp?
ANS: *One is female, the other is mail fee.*

What is the difference between a crazy hare and a counterfeit coin?
ANS: *One is a mad bunny, the other is bad money.*

What is the difference between a fisherman and a lazy schoolboy?
ANS: *One baits his hook, the other hates his book.*

What is the difference between an empty tube and a foolish Dutchman?
ANS: *One is a hollow cylinder, the other is a silly Hollander.*

What is the difference between a thief and a church bell?
ANS: *One steals from the people, the other peals from the steeple.*

What is the difference between a sewing machine and a kiss?
ANS: *One sews seams nice, the other seems so nice.*

What is the difference between a jeweler and a jailer?
ANS: *One sells watches, the other watches cells.*

What is the difference between a beautiful girl and a mouse?
ANS: *One charms the he's, the other harms the cheese.*

What is the difference between a cat and a comma?
ANS: One has its claws at the end of its paws, the other its pause at the end of its clause.

What is the difference between a chatterbox and a mirror?
ANS: One talks without reflecting, the other reflects without talking.

What is the difference between a glutton and a hungry man?
ANS: One eats too long, the other longs to eat.

What is the difference between a retired sailor and a blind man?
ANS: One cannot go to sea, the other cannot see to go.

What is the difference between a pianist and sixteen ounces of lead?
ANS: One pounds away, the other weighs a pound.

What is the difference between a hill and a pill?
ANS: One is hard to get up, the other is hard to get down.

What is the difference between an elevator and the man who runs it?
ANS: One is lowered to take passengers up, the other is hired to do it.

What is the difference between a summer dress in winter, and an extracted tooth?
ANS: One is too thin, the other is tooth out.

What is the difference between a man taking an oath of office, and a suit of castoff clothes?
ANS: One is sworn in, the other is worn out.

What is the difference between a sailor and the manager of a theater?
ANS: One likes to see a lighthouse, the other doesn't.

What is the difference between horse racing and going to church?
ANS: One makes men bet, the other makes them better.

What is the difference between a cow and a rickety chair?
ANS: One gives milk, the other gives way.

What is the difference between a well-dressed man and a tired dog?
ANS: *The man wears an entire suit, the dog just pants.*

What is the difference between a cat and a bullfrog?
ANS: *The cat has nine lives, but the bullfrog croaks every night.*

What is the difference between the manner of death of a barber and that of a sculptor?
ANS: *The barber curls up and dyes, while the sculptor makes faces and busts.*

What is the difference between a ballet dancer and a duck?
ANS: *One goes quick on her beautiful legs, the other goes quack on her beautiful eggs.*

What is the difference between a doe, an overpriced article, and a donkey?
ANS: *A doe is a deer, an overpriced article is too dear, and a donkey is you, dear.*

What is the difference between a man with an unnatural voice and one with unnatural teeth?
ANS: *One has a falsetto voice, the other a false set o' teeth.*

Why is this riddle the last in the book?
ANS: *Because there's none after it.*